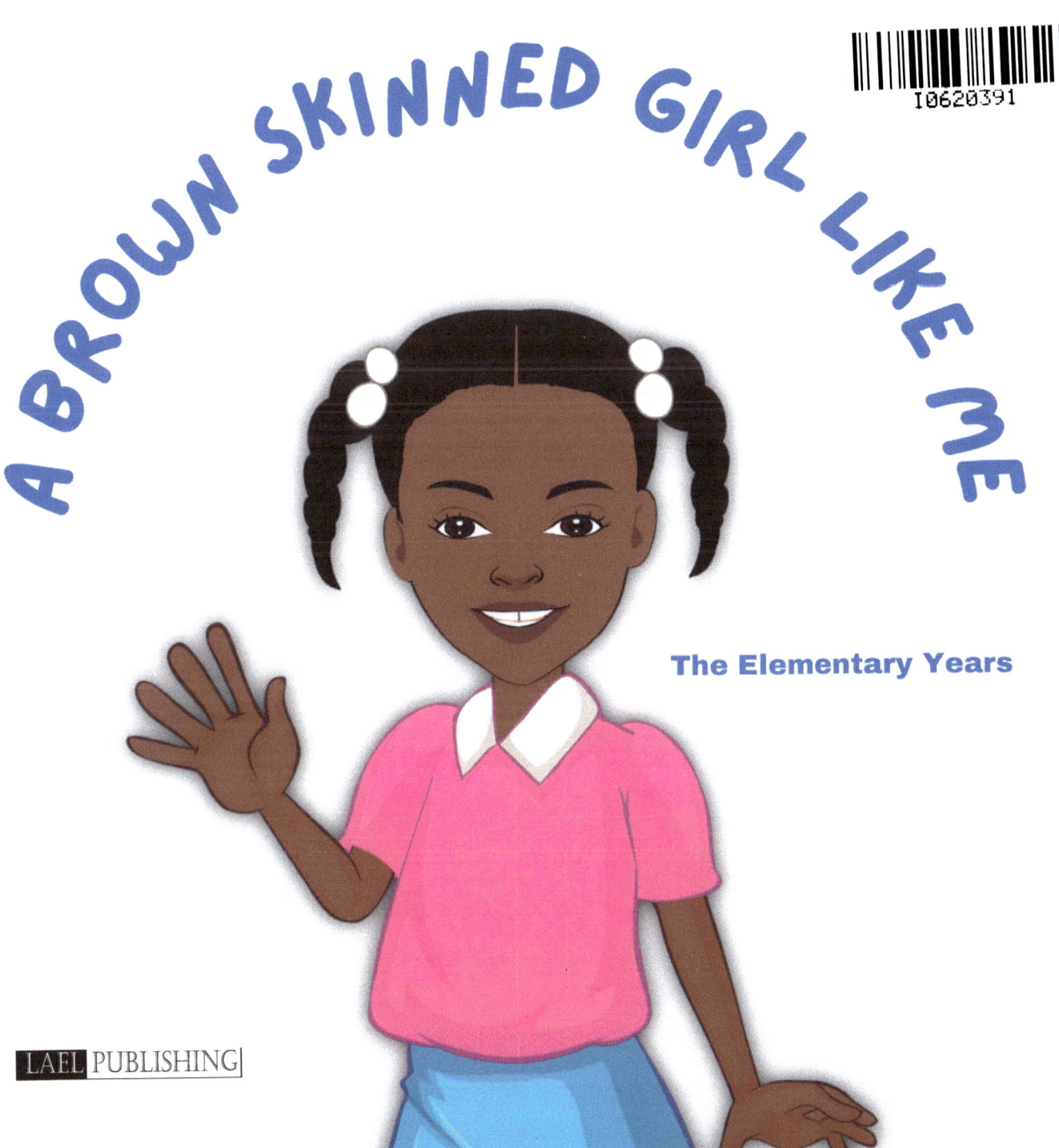

A BROWN SKINNED GIRL LIKE ME

The Elementary Years

LAEL PUBLISHING

A BROWN SKINNED GIRL LIKE ME

The Elementary Years

by Dr. Tammy Taylor Reginelli
Published by Lael Publishing, LLC
Winston Salem, North Carolina
www.LaelAgency.com

Paperback ISBN - 978-1-954433-22-9
Hardback ISBN - 978-1-954433-21-2

Author's Contact: DrTammy70@gmail.com

First Edition

Printed in the United States of America.

Dedication

So, who knew that a cute little brown-skinned girl like me would one day grow up to become Dr. Tammy Terell Taylor Reginelli? Here is the beginning of this journey.

This snippet from my early elementary years is meant to encourage young girls who may be wondering where they fit in this world. Don't worry, little brown-skinned girl- you are destined for greatness! I believe in you!

I dedicate this book to my grandmother, Louise Taylor Wilcher (Lula), for never letting me forget that the sky is the limit, and to my three beautiful children, who looked at me like the superstar I never knew was in their eyes could be. Mom loves you, Sierra, Briana, and Ashton. Mom, Thanks you for being my WHY!

I hope you enjoy this small token of appreciation for my family and everyone who believed in me.

Kindergarten and First Grade -The Wonder Years

Welcome to Elementary School! Wow, so you mean I must spend half of my day here? It looks like it might be a little bit of fun. I waited for the bus with my mom. who told me everything would be okay. And now, here I am, at the school, standing in this line, waiting for someone to tell us what to do. Wouldn't you know it. Here comes our teacher! Her name is Mrs. Eckols. She looks nice. I hope that she is nice. She is smiling. That is a good sign. She asked us to follow her, and all 20 of us did just that!

We enter the room and she shows us where to sit. She calls each of us by name as she points us to our seats. When she said my name, I was ready.

"Tammy, you will sit in the second seat on row number two," said Mrs. Eckols.

I rushed to my seat- I was so excited I couldn't wait for everyone to get settled! Even then, I was what some people called an over achiever. Others called me a smarty pants or teacher's pet, but I just called it being ready to learn! I was so eager to soak up every piece of information, like the cute little curly haired, brown-skinned sponge that I was.

That's when I started to notice the difference between me compared to the other students. Most of them wanted to run around the class and didn't want to pay attention. The teacher had to continue to point them back to their seats. It took a while to get them settled, and I started to feel a bit frustrated. Right. I know that is a big word for such a young girl, but my brain was ready for everything that came my way. Not only was my brain ready to do its own thing but I noticed that I was the only one who looked like me who really wanted to sit still long enough to point out colors, write our letters, and count as high as you could go. I also noticed that there were only a few of us in my assigned classroom. It was not until later that I learned that this was by design. It was planned by people much older than us!

You see, they had given us a test. This test was to show the adults the types of things that we already knew when we arrived to kindergarten. I had no idea that I had learned so much before I started school. My grandmother, Lula had done a good job keeping me busy with activities that helped my mind grow. I learned about groceries, chickens in the chicken coop, how to count money, my colors and numbers. I wanted to read so badly that I could barely wait and read, so read, I did!

Kindergarten and first grade flew by in a blur. I was excelling in all I was expected to learn in both grades. I could write, recite my alphabet, count, read, and more! Boy, was I excited about it all. Every day, I rushed home to tell Lula all about it! She listened to me as if I was the most important person in the world. You would have thought that I was the President who was giving the State of the Union, with a big speech, with the way that she listened to me. Her face showed so much joy and interest in what I had to say. When I finished, she would always tell me that I was very smart, but she didn't stop there. She asked me questions. Sometimes, I didn't know the answer right away, but that made me want to find out and come back with answers. That was the best part of talking to Lula. I always wanted to learn more and give her the answers. This is when the mind of this little, brown-skinned girl fell in love with learning new things or research as the grown-ups called it.

If soaking up information like a sponge had a picture, it would be me- a little, brown-skinned girl who was becoming the best that she should be at this age. This was the true beginning of years to come that were filled with the love of reading to learn. I could not put a book down! I had to know as much as this beautiful brain could handle. I would be willing to say that this is when I became a lifelong learner.

2nd grade - I Am A Big Girl Now

I am a big girl now, or so that's what I keep hearing! I'm in the second grade and ready to learn more than I have ever learned in my life! I couldn't get there fast enough. I could not wait for school to start again. Yes, I enjoyed summer, but I was ready to get back to school and excited to meet my new teacher and classmates. I felt it deep in my little, brown-skinned soul that this was going to be a fantastic year for everyone who worked hard.

9

I knew that I was going to work hard because I loved learning. It was my ticket out of my small town, a chance to gain new experiences, and to make something special of myself. You see, sometimes people from small towns will say you will not amount to anything. I was set on proving them wrong! Being from a small town does not mean that you won't become anything. It just means that you are from a small town and can still be everything that you want to be and even more than you expected. You can bet your last imaginary dollar that proving that this concept was a myth became one of my missions at an early age. This 2nd grader was going to be SOMEBODY!

When I entered my new classroom, I immediately noticed that my new teacher was interesting. At least, that's how I would describe her as a seven- year old, little me. The teacher would often randomly call on students to answer questions. That was just fine with me because I was always ready. We didn't need to waste any time on the formalities, the things adults added to make sure we got where we needed to go. Let the learning begin! This little brown- skinned girl was on fire!

I could write in cursive like a professional but please don't' tell my teacher that the closer that I was to becoming Dr. Tammy, this skill got a little lost in translation or at best it was rusty. Now, back to second grade. I had read every Nancy Drew novel that I could get my hands on and was eagerly waiting for the new ones to be released. I couldn't believe a young girl could solve so many mysteries. However, there was one thing that I noticed. She didn't look like me either. We were both very smart and could solve mysteries with very little help from others. However, the one thing that was missing in her stories was the melanin that I wished I could see.

That always made me think. I often wondered why the mysteries were never solved by anyone who looked like me. I know we were smart too but there was never a focus on US in many of the books in my school to include Nancy Drew. I didn't learn until later that this was also by design and on purpose. The school board hadn't approved enough books for us or by us. This was something that I did not understand until I was a teenager and started to understand things the way that adults would when I was little.

As I tried not to focus on this, I worked very hard in school. I could not let that stop me! I was usually the first to finish my math drills and was always eager to dive into reading passages.

Because I loved reading so much, I was always either the first or second to finish reading when we were assigned a reading passage. While speed was not always what the teacher was looking for, I still read pretty quickly.

In addition to speed, we were expected to do something called comprehend and answer questions about what it is that we had just read. We had to show the teacher that we could understand what we had just read. That's what she meant when she told us that we had to comprehend. Well, this smarty pants was sitting on the ready to answer the questions if by chance, I was called on. I noticed that I was not called on as often as I would like. Even back then, a little curly haired brown-skinned girl like me had to prove that she was just as smart— if not smarter— than my classmates. Guess what? I was up for the challenge!

You see, Grandma Lula had already told me that I was different in a good way. I also knew that from being around other people my age at home and in school. I wasn't everybody's cup of tea or favorite, even back then. That didn't bother me. What bothered me was that it wasn't always recognized in school. So, I worked even harder. I raised my hand more, did all of my homework, and even tried to help my classmates with their work.

Turns out, helping was not always encouraged. That is frowned upon by adults. The teachers didn't want us to help others because they needed to see what each student could do on their own. I wish someone had told me sooner! I just didn't want to wait for others to finish. I wanted them to hurry up so that I could learn more things. This part always tickles me because once I became an adult and had children of my own, one of them did the very same thing in first grade. Sometimes, you will just have to laugh. You will understand it more when you are a grown up. Let's get back to second grade.

Little Tammy was indeed little. I wasn't as tall as many of my classmates and I was more than likely underweight but still super cute. What I lacked in size, I made up for in smarts and charm. I was charming and witty for such a little thing. Even then, I could talk to adults like I was one of them. Turns out that was something that would be extremely helpful as an adult. The gift of gab or being able to talk to a perfect stranger about any and everything has helped me in so many ways. The second grader in me would never have guessed that or solved it in a mystery book. I could not have guessed that about my future even though I thought that I knew a lot!

As the year continued, I started to notice that the teacher called on me more and placed me in other groups with students who were considered to be smart kids. However, these students didn't look like me either. That was not a big deal, but I found it interesting and wanted to know more. I started to see that as a pattern. These groups were not made up of little brown skinned girls like me. I could not help but notice it.

I began to wonder why there weren't more brown-skinned children in my group. I learned that many factors affected our groupings, and it wasn't always about our abilities. As an adult, who became an educator, I learned that many brown- skinned children were overlooked based on teacher biases or how teachers felt about the child.

As for the groups during 2nd grade, we were placed in the accelerated readers' group. It seems that those of us who really liked to read were reading more books. We read at least ten books each week and answered all the comprehension questions correctly. Boy, was Grandma Lula proud! I hoped that other children who looked like me had the same type or similar encouragement at home. Some did, and some didn't. So, I took it upon myself to encourage them. I cheered for others. I wanted us all to succeed!

The students in the accelerated readers' group got recognized in class and were given certificates. At the end of the year, we were recognized by the entire second grade for our hard work. I wore the cutest outfit, and my hair was in two ponytails tied with pink bows on each side. You could not tell me anything at all. Here I stood tall and proud, for not just being recognized, but because I was, a little brown- skinned girl who was as smart as everyone else! I didn't like hearing that I was "smart for a brown girl." I wanted people to simply say I was smart. It was almost as if I was not expected to be as smart as everyone else. It also turned out that everyone else that people were talking about did not look like me. No worries! This was only more fuel to get me going in a direction that would one day lead to success. I wanted to shine brightly in every part of my life. I was determined!

This was just the beginning!

Third grade- Power to the People

This was definitely the beginning. I had made up my mind to be the best I could be, not just for myself but for all the kids who looked like me. I started third grade year with pajazz and smarts. I was determined to read even more books and tackle even more math problems. The world was going to know that everyone including little, brown-skinned girls like me were smart and not "smarty pants"!

In third grade, we began getting math problems that were full of words. Ugh! I really loved reading, but why did math have to be so wordy? Whose idea was it to mix words with numbers? Our teacher told us to focus on the important words. I wondered, "Aren't all words important?" Here I was thinking hard in the third grade! Thankfully, she finally showed us how to weed out or get rid of the not so important words. Well, thank goodness because, I thought each word should be a focus. We were taught that we needed to pick out the key words. Once I learned that I could remove all words that didn't have anything to do with exactly how many apples were left, without worrying about who went to the store or how long it took them to get there in the car, I was ready! From that moment on, word problems became easy.

Oddly enough, this was not the case for everyone. But not everyone felt the same way. My teacher chose a few of us to help people in our math groups during center time. We had a group leader who would read the problem out loud to everyone and then helped them to solve the problems. I was proud to be one of the group leaders! Helping others reach their math goals felt amazing. You see, we even helped the teacher develop and set math goals for the first nine weeks. If I could help my classmates succeed, they could move up to another math group. How cool was that?

Unfortunately, not everyone shared my zeal or the newly found love of excitement for word problems. Some of them wanted to talk or goof off instead of working. Even my friends want to talk or play around when they are supposed to be doing their work. Here I was again, frustrated! Now, I needed to find a way to keep them on task. I could not let this get out of hand. So, I reminded them that the sooner that we finished, the sooner we could get to recess. I didn't really care about getting to recess at that time, but it was a great motivator for my classmates! They focused and worked so hard on the problems that they almost forgot about recess. Well, they forgot about recess all the way until the teacher said, "Time's up. Recess time."

Then, they flew out of the classroom like the school was on fire. So much for being a motivator. I would try again the next day. That's how it went at least twice a week during our math center time.

Reading was still my passion. Nancy Drew and I had mysteries to solve, and we continued our adventures through my fifth-grade year. However, while in the third grade, I had to read even more than ten books a week. Now, I needed an adult at home to sign off on my reading to prove that I had read the books. Turns out, some students were not honest about how many books that they were reading each week. They would go to the library and write down the titles of the books to get credit without reading the books. I think that they forgot that they also had to answer those pesky comprehension questions afterward. That's how they got caught or as some people would call it "busted". I wanted to laugh, but I knew it wasn't a good idea, so I kept it to myself. It was kind of clever, but not the greatest plan for anyone. Their parents were called, and note was sent home to be signed. Boy, was I glad that I liked reading!

That same year, my parents received a note saying I was "too intelligent" to remain in third grade. Yes, they used that big word. I looked it up in the dictionary back in second grade! My parents met with the principal, my teacher, and the school counselor to talk about not only skipping me up a couple of grades but to also allow me to join a special group for advanced students, called Quest. I wanted to do both. However, my parents were not sold.

They listened to all the information that was given to them and decided I should stay in third grade. They also decided not to allow me to join Quest. Here were their reasons. Yes, I was really, really smart, but I was also still very small. The fifth graders would be much taller than me and might pick on me because of my size.

According to my parents, kids don't care about how smart you are when they decide to bully you. They decided against Quest because it would further isolate me from other students who looked like me. Being in the advance reading and math groups already provided me with what my parents called unnecessary isolation to some extent. While I did not agree with my parents, I had to follow their lead and finish out the rest of the year as a third grader with the big brain.

I finished with a bang, earning all A's and one B. The B was because I was rebelling a little bit for not being moved up. I talked a little more than I should to others who weren't finishing their work. I felt like I was doing something important. I tried to help them. I must have been the Angela Davis of the third grade and taking a stand against what I considered an injustice. She was a very important person in our history who had many things to say and now I felt almost as important. Most importantly, I survived and moved on to the fourth grade. However, my new motto, thanks to Angela Davis, that I still use today was used by me back then, Power to the People!

Fourth Grade Year

I am now a fourth grade student and ready to take on the world! Math problems were coming rapid fire and reading was required. This year, we had two teachers instead of one! We switched between these two teachers for our main subjects like math, reading, social studies, and science, plus we had a teacher just for PE. We had heavier books than we had ever had. The teachers seemed stricter this year, but I was ready for that. They had no idea how strict things were at home. I laughed inside at what the teachers called strict. I liked having "rituals and routines", as the teachers called them. Every morning, they posted our schedule for the day and made sure that they would stick to it . without fail. We were rarely a minute late moving from one subject or class to another. I didn't understand then, but later as a teacher myself, I understood the importance of every minute that we had to teach our students. We could not waste one valuable second of that precious instructional time.

This little girl was ready. My freshly wrapped books were also ready for transition. I had taken the time to use the finest of paper bags to make my very own custom book covers and I had a brand new blue Trapper Keeper notebook with five dividers on the inside. Even back then Royal Blue was my favorite color and still is. You could not tell me anything!

I watched the clock before each transition, finishing my work early but I didn't try to get out of my seat to help others because this was still frowned upon. Keep in mind that nobody said anything about helping them on the ride to and from school. This girl was going to do her part in helping others to succeed. Yes indeed!

Fourth grade wasn't too hard. Everyone was working harder and making new friends, but, in this process, I learned that girls in the fourth grade didn't really like it if you showed people just how smart you were. I learned that these girls sometimes wanted to dim your light a little bit. I learned that this was not going away any time soon, so I had to make a choice between being smart or having a bunch of friends. I decided I didn't need too many friends; true friends would love me for who I am!

That year, I lost a lot of friends, or what I now know to be called "associates." But what I gained that year was something even better: self-love and respect. I had chosen to stand tall in my beautiful melanin-filled skin and embraced the truest version of my nine-year-old self, even if it took a lot of courage. Wow. I realized the guts that took much later in life. Fourth grade flew by! I could count on one hand how many true friends I made. A small number, but I learned that was best for me then and even now as an adult. It is better to have a few true friends you can count on whenever you need them instead of a lot of people who aren't really there for you when you need them.

I noticed that there was an even larger division between people of color and those who did not look like us based on our skin colors. Not only were we separated into groups by the teachers that was designed to focus on our skill levels, but the children had also routinely divided themselves by color lines which worried me I was taught not to see lines of color among people, only the colors in the crayon boxes. Here, I was a nine-year-old diplomat. This trait turned out to be helpful as a grown-up, but not all children in the fourth grade would care about diplomacy. Some kids didn't like my efforts to bring everyone together, but I didn't give up! I continued to focus on getting good grades and showed others that we could ALL get along. I did not win a Nobel Peace Prize but that year, but I would not give up hope.

As my ponytails grew longer and the melanin in my skin was really popping, some kids started to notice my outer beauty more than my inner smarts. The fact that I was what many called smart began to be less noticeable for some people because another lesson that I learned in fourth grade is that people begin to look at your outer beauty instead of your inner beauty. Well, I bet you already know how I handled that. I worked extra hard to focus on my inner beauty and to let that light shine I didn't give up on using my brain to learn new things and to help others. I did not focus on the outer beauty as others did. However, I learned that many others did and that concept opened doors for some people and not others.

This really made me think even more about how to focus on being a good student and person. I decided to focus on being a good student and a good friend, making sure no one thought I got special treatment because of how I looked. I know. You may wonder what nine-year-old thinks this way? Well, I did! I was and still am different, and that's perfectly okay. Being different does not mean better. It simply means that you are different and my version of different just meant that I was willing to be my true self all those years ago without knowing that could have a long lasting positive impact on others. I was being ME! I realized it was important to let my light shine, both inside and out. I was ready for whatever came next! I just thought that the impact would be temporary or short lived but positive. This girl was still on FIRE!

Fifth Grade Year

Time flew by. I was no longer standing at the end of that long dirt road in the mornings with my mom while we waited for my cousin, the bus driver to pick me up. Now, I was allowed to go without her but I had to walk with my little brother who is two years younger than me. Yes. I left that out earlier. I was a big sister and a role model for him too. Whew. The pressure was on! I had to show him how to stand there and wait for the bus without talking to any strangers passing by on the main road. I think that I did a pretty good job. However, one day he decided to start throwing rocks at cars. and the bus driver saw it. Both of us got in trouble. Ten-year-old me was highly upset with him and honestly, I might still be a little mad that I got in trouble for his rock throwing. It is a good story to tell and it is a part of who I am in this world today.

That incident taught me that you can be unintentionally or accidentally be involved in something you didn't mean to, and you have to figure out how to deal with the negative consequences that might be a result of that particular incident. In this case, I pleaded my case and managed to avoid punishment that I did not deserve. Yet another life lesson about being honest and true to myself and others. My brother might not have liked it at the time, but we moved on. So, back to the fifth grade.

Fifth grade was a little harder. We still had two teachers and a PE teacher. Recess time was longer and the girls my age were even meaner. I got into my very first fight in the bathroom with a girl who was supposed to be my friend. It turned out, she was envious of me being called a smart girl and she didn't want her friends to be my friends. This initially confused me because she looked like me. She was a brown skinned girl ! I didn't understand why we couldn't all be smart and friends at the same

25

time. That lesson took me a little longer to learn than the other lessons that I learned in elementary school. Girls could be meaner than I ever imagined!

Despite all of that, I focused on school. I read more books than I ever had read. I did all my homework as always and even helped others with theirs. I learned the skill of being funny when needed. It turns out that being smart and funny was something that people liked. Who knew that being funny helped too? Everyone could relate to a good joke, whether they were little brown-skinned girls like me or not. The teachers and students could use a little more fun. No. I was definitely not the class clown as it was called back in the day. We already had someone who had been identified as the class clown but I really did not like that name for him. He was a little brown-skinned boy who could have been my brother. It broke my heart to hear him being called that name. I think that you know what came next. It was my mission to help him with his work. I had figured out he was acting that way because he didn't know the information for our lessons. Whenever, the teachers called on him to answer questions that he didn't know the answer to, he would say or do something he thought was funny. He didn't realize that it wasn't helping him at all, in fact it was getting in the way of the rest of us learning.

This is where I had to put my foot down so to speak. One day, I talked to him on the bus. I said I liked his jokes, but that I liked learning even more. You're probably wondering what happened to the diplomacy that I mentioned earlier. Well, in that moment, it went out of the window. Our teachers had made it very clear to us that we had some very important state tests that we needed to pass before we could go to the sixth grade. Nothing was standing in my way of going to middle school! We had a little tough love conversation, and he just looked at me for a minute before he responded. I think he thought I was a little silly for talking to him about how he acts in school since I was not an adult. Once he got past that, he agreed to acting a little less silly in class so that he and the rest of us could learn without distractions. I had to beat him in a foot race on the playground the next day. or there would not be a deal between us. I looked at him and accepted his offer not having any idea how I would beat him in a race.

When I got home that day, I made sure to eat all of my vegetables, just like Grandma Lula insisted. Nothing new. Grandma Lula required it. We always had to eat our vegetables, or we could not have dessert. I loved her hot apple or peach turnovers. I finish dinner, did my homework. I watched a couple after school tv shows and then it was time to clean up, take a bath, and go to bed. I didn't

sleep much that night, knowing I had accepted a challenge I more than likely would lose. That didn't stop me from hopping up the next morning like I was Florence Joyner Griffith, or "Flo Jo" as your parents might have called her. I quickly got dressed and put on what was my best pair of sneakers. Now, if you knew us, you knew that we didn't have a lot of money so, my best pair of sneakers didn't have a name brand on them but they would have to work for the day.

I get on the bus and start the journey to school. I felt determined. Since we lived next door to the bus driver, we were always the first children on the bus. The route to school continues and I ride with a nervous smile on my face. When we got to my classmate's bus stop, I didn't see him there, so I thought he might have chickened out. But just as the bus was about to pull off, he walked up. You guessed it. I was a little bit disappointed and suddenly a little scared. In class, focusing on my work wasn't too difficult because I had made up my mind that no matter what happened, I would still work hard on my school work. Learning was always my go to for peace.

We had lunch and then we went to recess. It turned out he had told everyone who would listen that he had challenged me to a race, and that he would run so fast that they would see smoke coming off of his shoes while leaving me in the dust. Everyone was lined up and ready to see my defeat. I can't say that I blame them because I was still kind of little in size, but my legs had gotten a little longer over the summer. My secret weapon was that I ran races with my younger brother and a bunch of boy cousins often and won a few times too, which I had forgotten until that very moment. Talk about a boost in my confidence.

I had to run from one end of the playground to the other. There were two classmates at the beginning and two at the end who were waiting to tell everyone who won the race.
When it was time to race, we got down into our racing positions.

"Ready, Set, Go!" shouted one of our classmates. As soon as we heard the word "go", I took off like a rocket. So did he! He was running extremely fast. I could hear his feet hitting the ground with each step, but I dared not look in his direction. I had watched enough races to know not to get distracted or look at the competition, so I just ran. I ran so fast and hard that I didn't realize I had come to the end of the playground.

I heard somebody say, "She won!" I thought that maybe someone else had jumped in the race with us and I didn't know it. Nope. I WON! I was so scared to lose that I actually won.

Beyond Elementary School

Being different was a superpower in elementary school, and it helped me to grow into the pretty cool adult I am today! I'm proud to be an Army Veteran and a mom of three amazing adult children.

Being a smart brown-skinned girl shaped who I am. Remember, don't give up! Don't get discouraged when people think you need to work twice as hard as others who do not look like you. Don't be sad because there are times that you might be overlooked just because of your skin color. Don't you dare let anyone dim your light because being a brown skinned girl is such a blessing that nobody else can experience! For every failure or delayed successful moment know that there are twice as many wonderful moments of success to follow.

Be sure to love yourself and the skin you are in. Now that you know just how special you are, be on the lookout for the next book in the ***A Brown Skinned Girl Like Me*** series.

Much love!
Dr. Tammy

About the Author

Dr. Tammy Reginelli is a seasoned educator, training specialist, program manager, and travel business owner, who has recently embarked on a new journey as an author. As the proud mother of three amazing adult children—Sierra, Briana, and Ashton—she is inspired daily by their growth and accomplishments. Driven to be a positive role model, she continually strives for personal growth and aims to show her children that no goal is too impossible to reach. In her spare time, she enjoys spending time with her kids, dancing, and, of course, writing. She firmly believes that where you come from doesn't define where you're going in life.